Mama's
Rules for Livin'

by
Mamie McCullough

Tulsa, Oklahoma

Mama's Rules for Livin'
ISBN 1-56292-340-4
Copyright © 1995 by Mamie McCullough
305 Spring Creek Village
P.O. Box 372
Dallas, Texas 75248
(800)255-4226

Published by Honor Books, Inc.
P.O. Box 55388
Tulsa, Oklahoma 74155

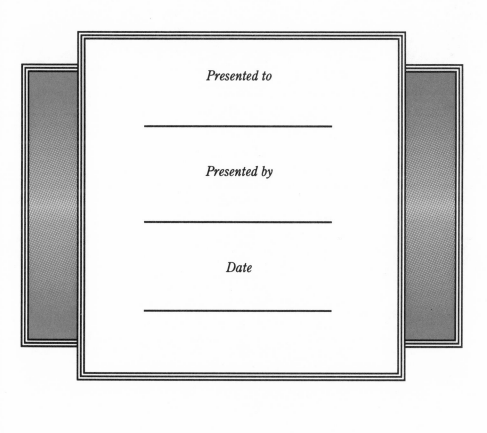

Presented to

_____

Presented by

_____

Date

_____

Introduction

We all need rules and regulations in order to grow into healthy individuals. As children, these are handed down to us by our parents or significant others. I was fortunate to have a wonderful mother who was not formally educated, but who had much wisdom. Mother raised me, my five sisters, and my three brothers on four basic rules:

Go to Church   Love Others   Stay Clean   Work Hard

As I have raised my three children, these have been the "unwritten" rules for my home as well. If you are a person who has not had a good and caring parent then *Mama's Rules for Livin'* will mean even more to you. The ideas in this book have worked for me, now I would like to share these nuggets with you and those in your home.

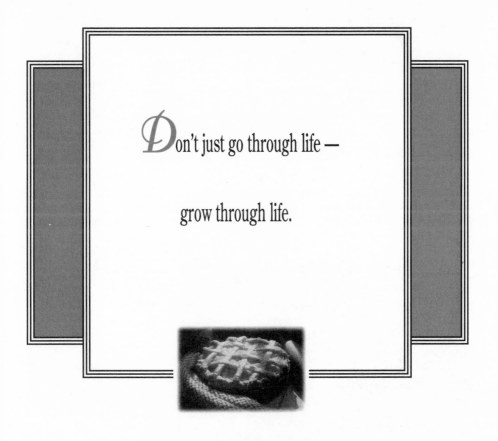

$\mathcal{D}$on't just go through life —

grow through life.

····**Mama's Rules for Livin'**····

7.

*N*ever let your burdens paralyze
your progress.

*T*rue success is learning what to
do with failure.

····I Believe In You····

*N*o matter what you've done...

I believe in you!

····Mama's Rules for Livin'····

9.

We make our habits, then
in turn our habits make us.

Little things make a big difference.

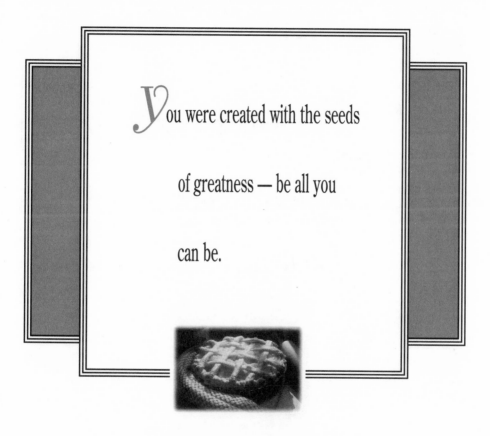

$\mathcal{Y}$ou were created with the seeds

of greatness — be all you

can be.

Winners develop the habit of

doing those things that losers

refuse to do.

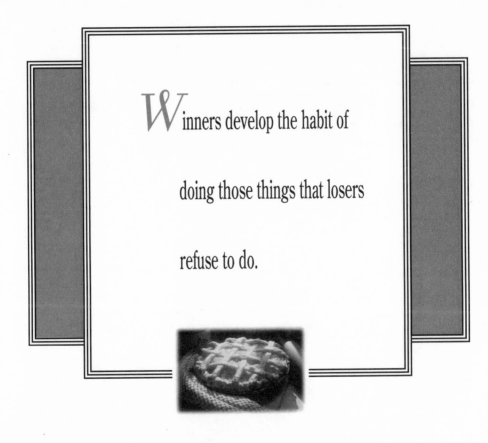

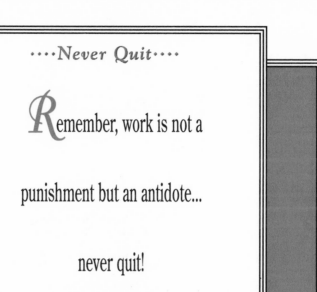

···· Never Quit ····

*R*emember, work is not a

punishment but an antidote...

never quit!

···· **Mama's Rules for Livin'** ····

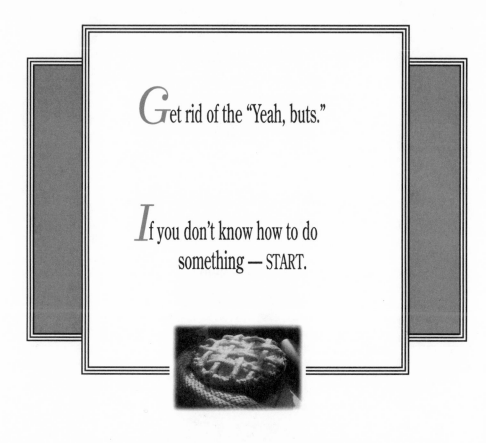

*G*et rid of the "Yeah, buts."

*I*f you don't know how to do
something — START.

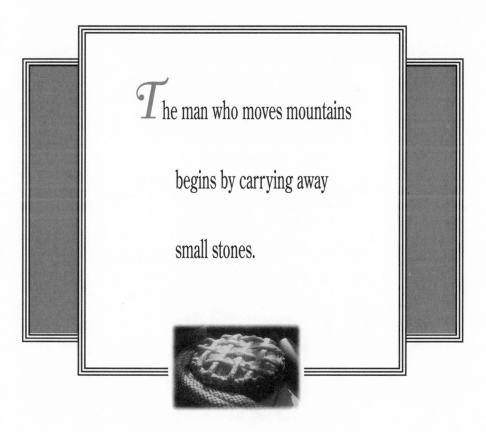

*T*he man who moves mountains

begins by carrying away

small stones.

15.

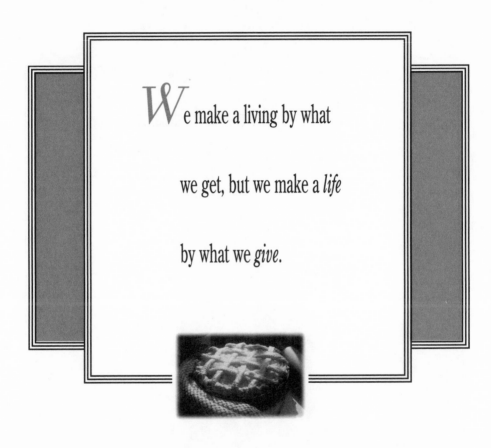

$\mathcal{W}$e make a living by what

we get, but we make a *life*

by what we *give*.

····Mama's Rules for Livin'····

Give the best you've got, and

you may get kicked in the teeth...

give the best you've got anyway!

*P*eople don't plan to fail —
they fail to plan.

*G*oals are dreams with deadlines.

*I*t is not because things are difficult

that we do not dare. It is

because we do not dare that

things are difficult.

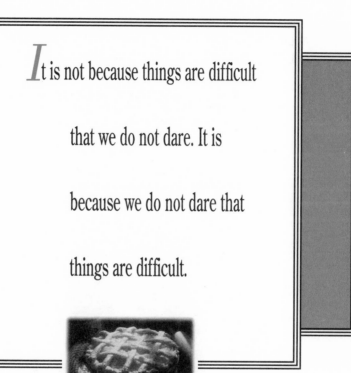

·····Mama's Rules for Livin'·····

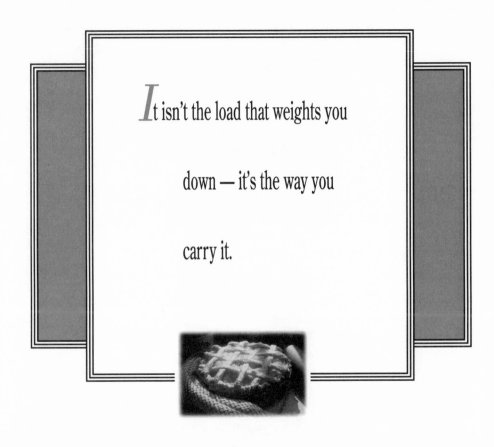

*I*t isn't the load that weights you

down — it's the way you

carry it.

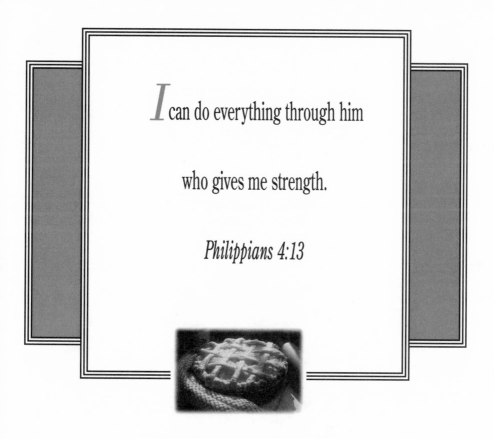

I can do everything through him

who gives me strength.

Philippians 4:13

····Mama's Rules for Livin'····

*I*t is never right to do wrong.

*I*t is never wrong to do right.

····Mama's Rules for Livin'····

22.

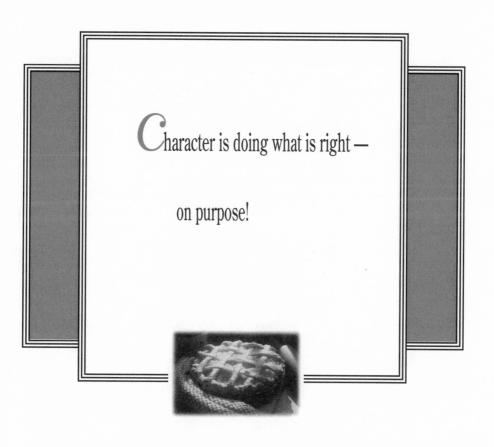

Character is doing what is right —

on purpose!

A person wrapped up in himself

makes a very small package.

····**Mama's Rules for Livin'**····

24.

W hen you become a parent

remember: Children are sent

through us — not to us.

*Y*ou do not have to like
everything a person does
in order to love him.

*R*espect the rights, customs,
and differences of others.

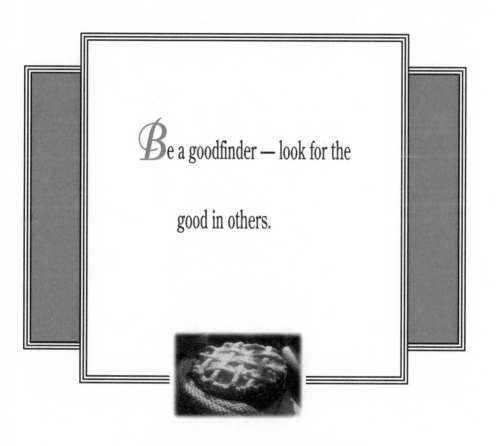

*B*e a goodfinder — look for the

good in others.

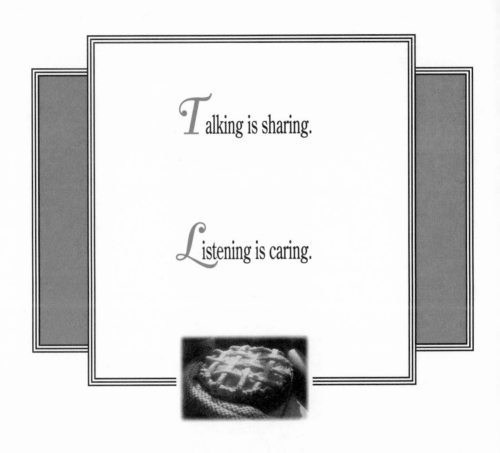

*T*alking is sharing.

*L*istening is caring.

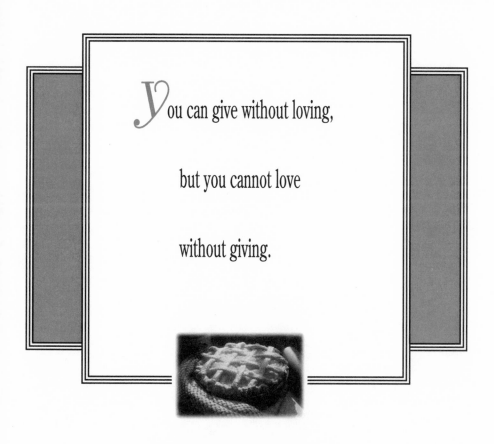

$\mathcal{Y}$ou can give without loving,

but you cannot love

without giving.

*I*f you want to be an original,

be yourself.

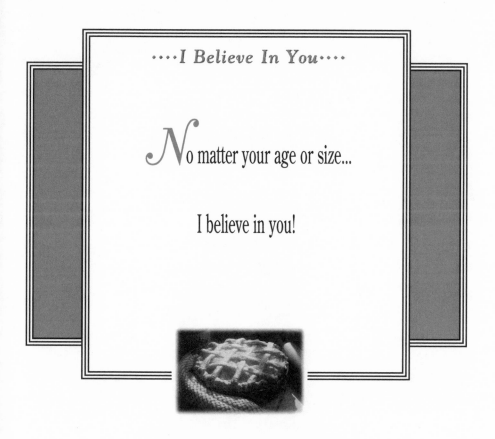

····*I Believe In You*····

*N*o matter your age or size...

I believe in you!

····Mama's Rules for Livin'····

31.

*G*od does not promise to leave
us comfortable, but He will
never leave us comfortless.

*F*aith is seeing a rainbow in
each tear.

····*Mama's Rules for Livin'*····

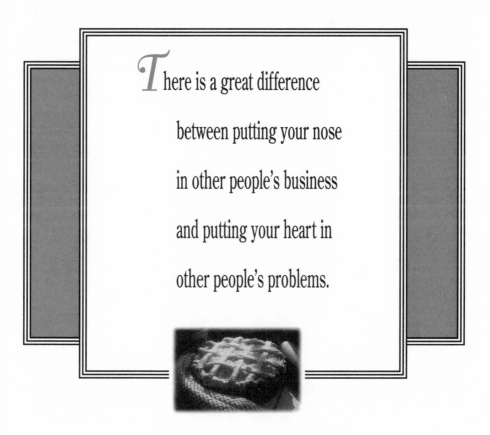

*T*here is a great difference

between putting your nose

in other people's business

and putting your heart in

other people's problems.

····Mama's Rules for Livin'····

33.

Winners are not "why-ners."

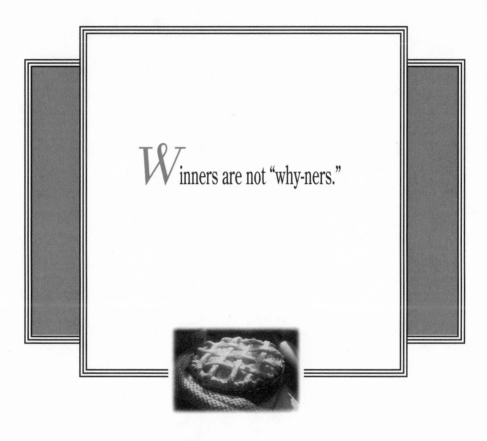

····Never Quit····

*E*ven when the odds

seem against you...

never quit!

····Mama's Rules for Livin'····

35.

*A*s we see people, so we tend to
treat them.

*A*s we treat people, often they
become.

····Mama's Rules for Livin'····

36.

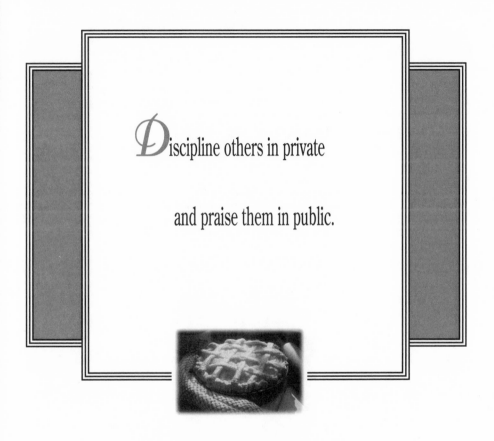

*D*iscipline others in private

and praise them in public.

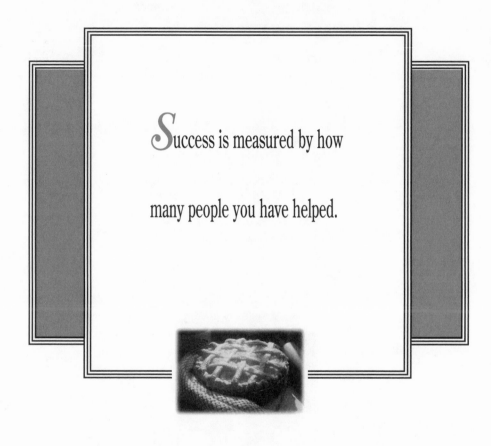

*S*uccess is measured by how

many people you have helped.

····Do Good Anyway····

When you do good, people may

accuse you of selfish ulterior

motives...do good anyway!

····Mama's Rules for Livin'····

39.

*W*hen you sling mud, you're
just losing ground.

*S*implify your life — shake off
the hurt, bitterness,
and bad feelings.

••••*Mama's Rules for Livin'*••••

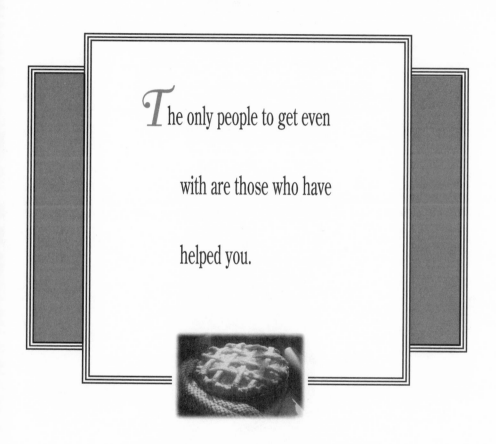

$\mathcal{T}$he only people to get even

with are those who have

helped you.

····Mama's Rules for Livin'····

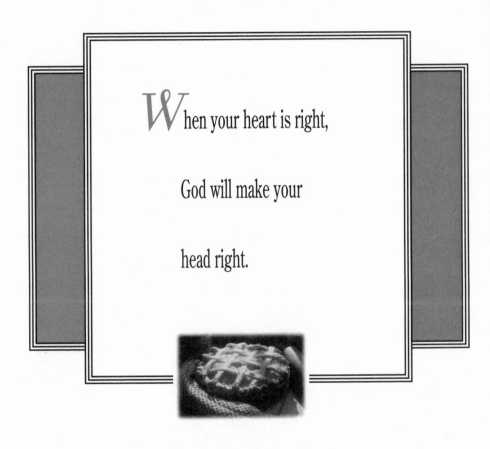

When your heart is right,

God will make your

head right.

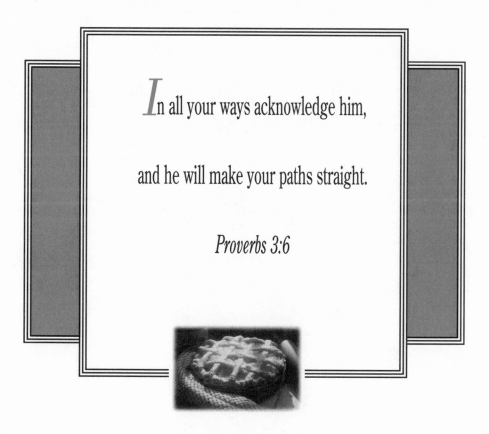

*I*n all your ways acknowledge him,

and he will make your paths straight.

Proverbs 3:6

····*Mama's Rules for Livin'*····

*D*o not complain about what
you permit.

*T*ake steps to overcome
your failures.

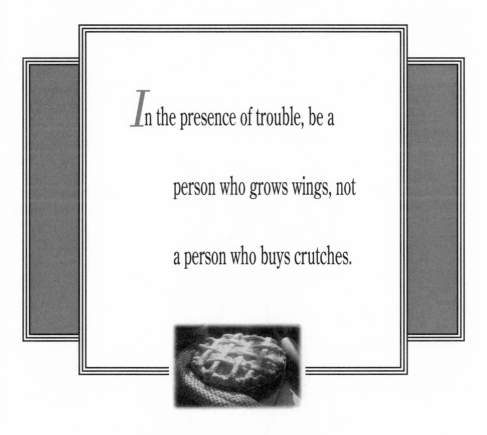

*I*n the presence of trouble, be a

person who grows wings, not

a person who buys crutches.

····**Mama's Rules for Livin'**····

45.

*S*tay alert for opportunity.

When you become a parent

remember: To be in your children's

memories tomorrow, you have to

be in their lives today.

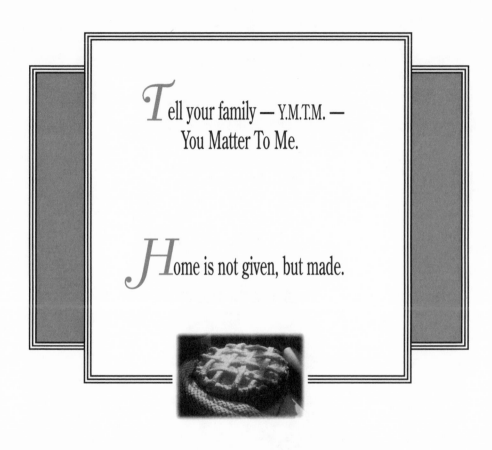

*T*ell your family — Y.M.T.M. —
You Matter To Me.

*H*ome is not given, but made.

····*Mama's Rules for Livin'*····

$\mathcal{L}$earn to laugh at yourself,

and you will never run out

of things to laugh about.

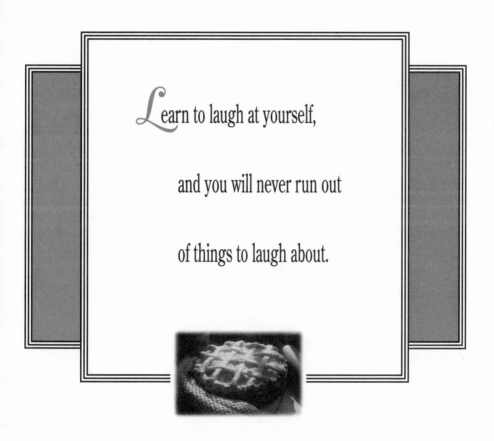

$\mathcal{P}$ull together at home as a team.

$\mathcal{W}$hen you help your family,
you help yourself.

*C*harity begins at home —

but it doesn't stay there.

·····*Mama's Rules for Livin'*·····

51.

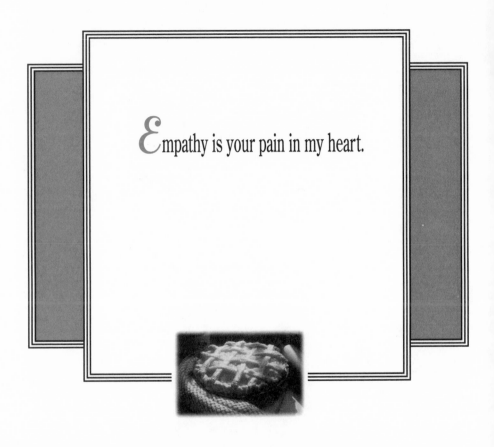

*E*mpathy is your pain in my heart.

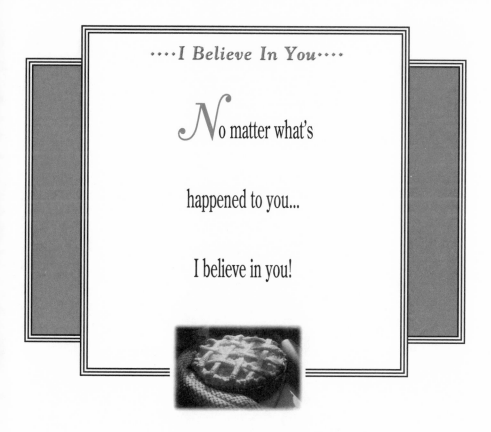

····*I Believe In You*····

*N*o matter what's

happened to you...

I believe in you!

····**Mama's Rules for Livin'**····

$\mathcal{D}$on't condemn, criticize,
or complain.

$\mathcal{F}$ix the problem —
not the blame.

····*Mama's Rules for Livin'*····

*I*f you speak kind words, you will

hear kind echoes.

····Mama's Rules for Livin'····

♪♪.

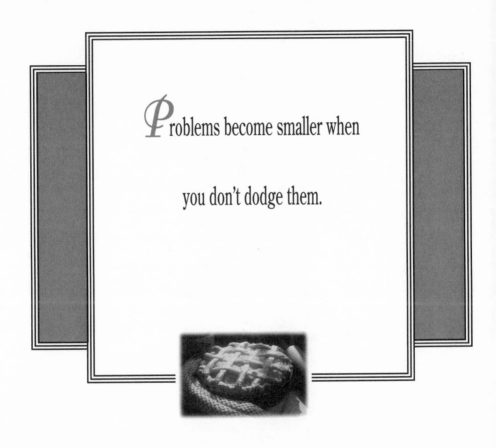

$\mathcal{P}$roblems become smaller when

you don't dodge them.

····Never Quit····

*P*roblems are only opportunities

in work clothes...

never quit!

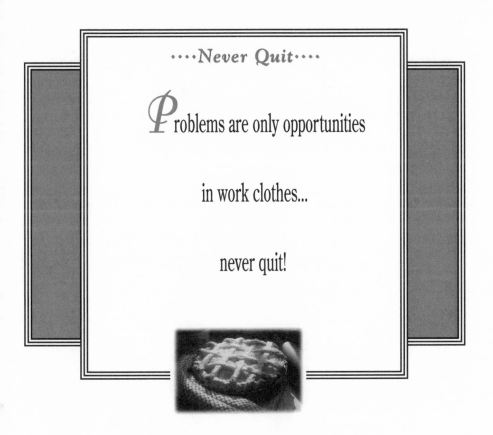

A gem cannot be polished
without friction.

T he child of God cannot be
perfected without adversity.

····Mama's Rules for Livin'····

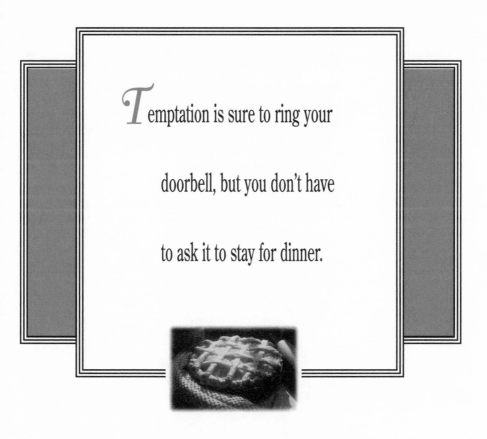

*T*emptation is sure to ring your

doorbell, but you don't have

to ask it to stay for dinner.

$\mathcal{Y}$ou don't have to *feel* good to

do good.

····**Mama's Rules for Livin'**····

60.

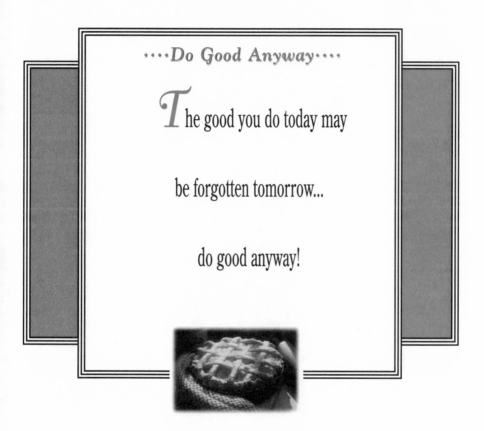

····Do Good Anyway····

*T*he good you do today may

be forgotten tomorrow...

do good anyway!

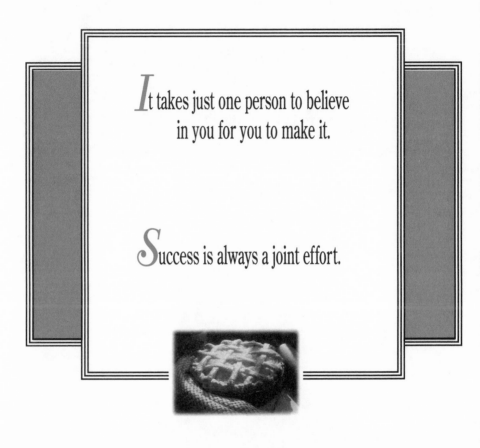

*I*t takes just one person to believe
in you for you to make it.

*S*uccess is always a joint effort.

True friends are those who,

when you've made a fool of

yourself, don't think you've

done a permanent job.

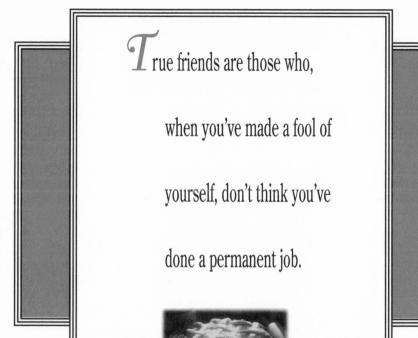

····Mama's Rules for Livin'····

63.

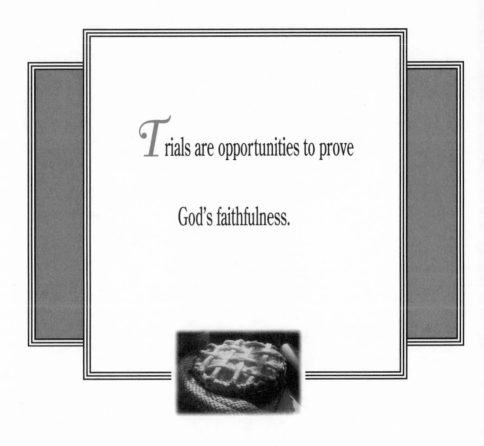

$\mathcal{T}$rials are opportunities to prove

God's faithfulness.

Come near to God and he will

come near to you.

James 4:8a

····*Mama's Rules for Livin'*····

65.

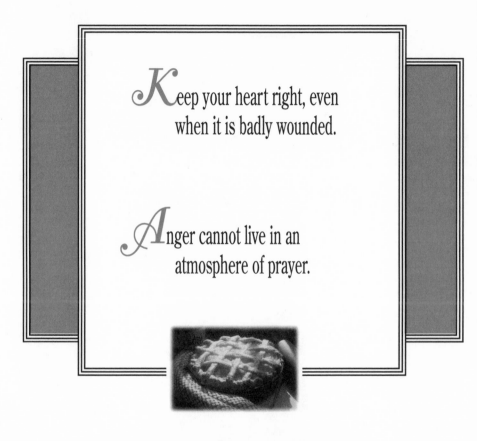

$\mathcal{K}$eep your heart right, even
when it is badly wounded.

$\mathcal{A}$nger cannot live in an
atmosphere of prayer.

····Mama's Rules for Livin'····

$\mathcal{L}$earn to say kind things because

nobody ever resents them.

$\mathcal{Y}$ou can regain your integrity;

it's never too late to start.

*W*hen you become a parent

remember: Don't allow anything in

your life that you don't want

reproduced in your children's lives.

···· Mama's Rules for Livin' ····

69.

*T*oday is all you have, so live
each day to its fullest.

*L*earn to manage time, energy,
and money.

$\mathcal{P}$ay who you owe, what you owe,

when you owe it.

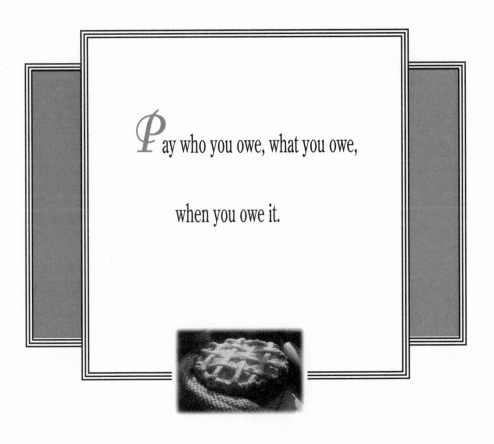

····**Mama's Rules for Livin'**····

$\mathcal{P}$ut gratitude in your attitude.

$\mathcal{F}$ocus on your haves, not your have nots.

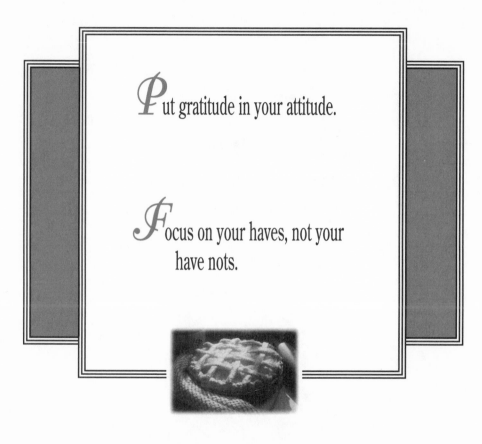

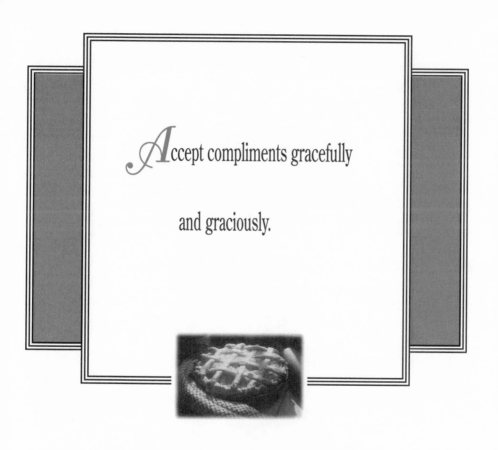

*A*ccept compliments gracefully

and graciously.

More and bigger is not

always better.

····I Believe In You····

*N*o matter your position

or lack of one...

I believe in you!

····Mama's Rules for Livin'····

75.

*D*ream the big dream and go
for it.

I *can* is a way of life.

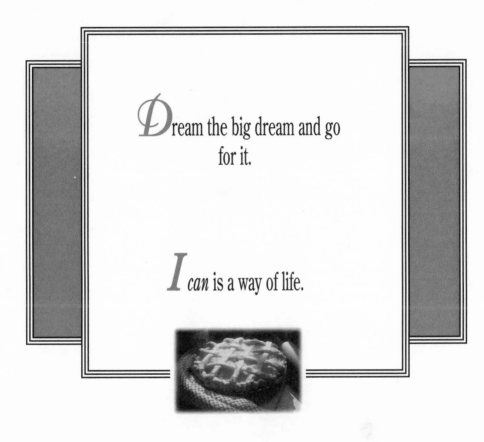

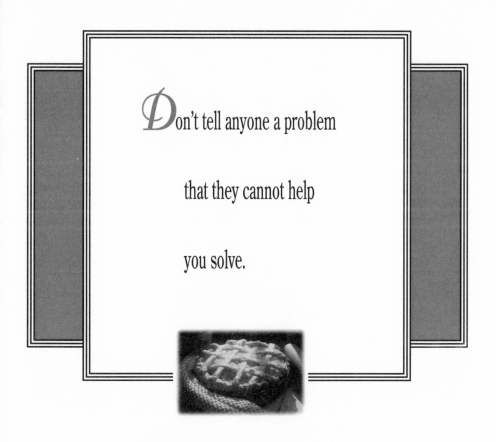

$\mathcal{D}$on't tell anyone a problem

that they cannot help

you solve.

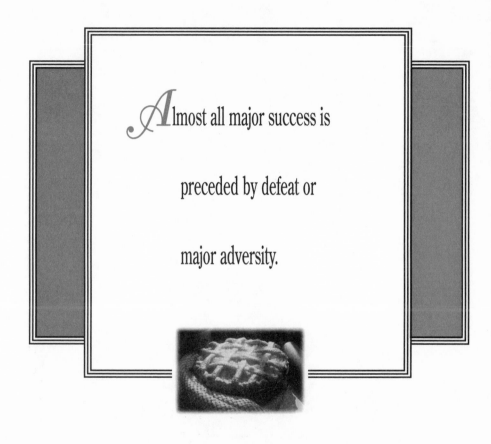

*A*lmost all major success is

preceded by defeat or

major adversity.

$\mathscr{F}$ailure is temporary...

never quit!

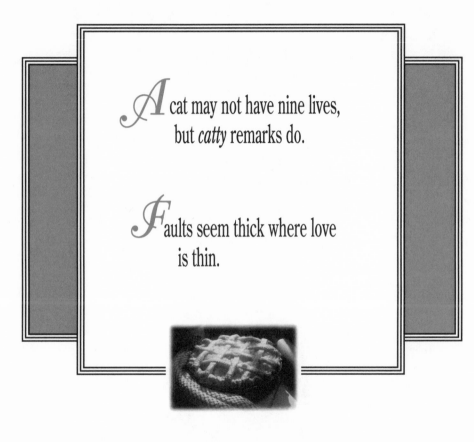

A cat may not have nine lives,
but *catty* remarks do.

F aults seem thick where love
is thin.

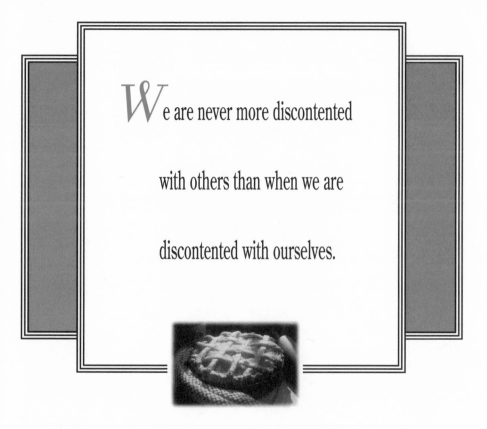

We are never more discontented

with others than when we are

discontented with ourselves.

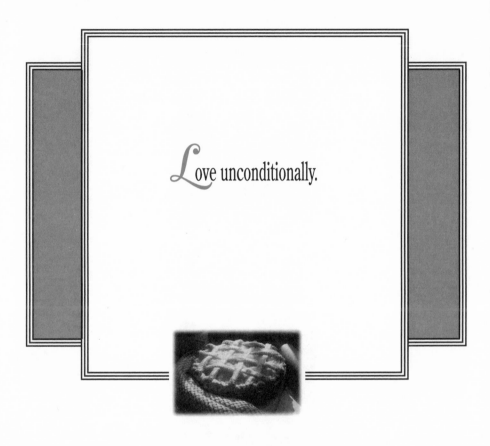

*L*ove unconditionally.

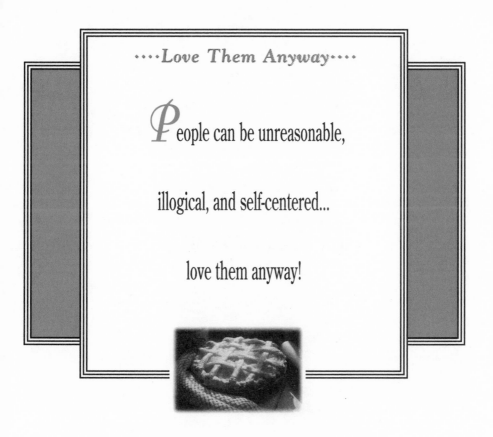

····Love Them Anyway····

*P*eople can be unreasonable,

illogical, and self-centered...

love them anyway!

····Mama's Rules for Livin'····

83.

*T*he power to destroy or build
lies in the power of the tongue.

*B*e careful what you say
to others.

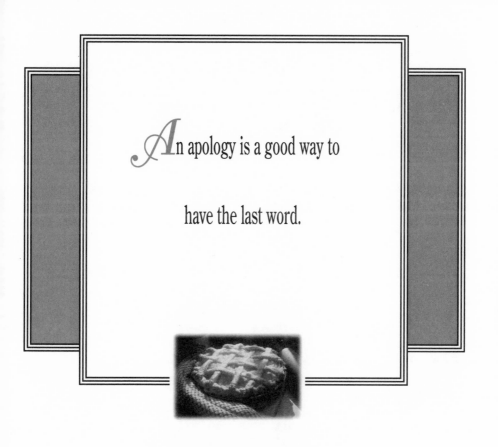

$\mathcal{A}$n apology is a good way to

have the last word.

····**Mama's Rules for Livin'**····

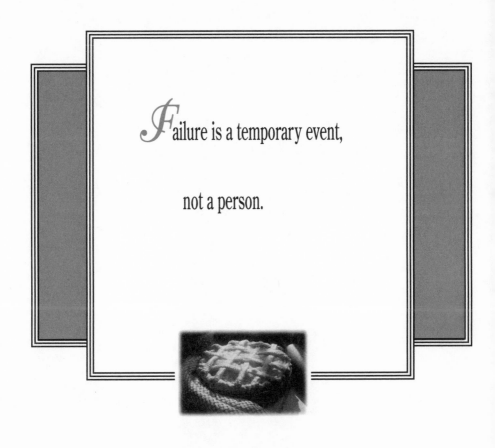

*F*ailure is a temporary event,

not a person.

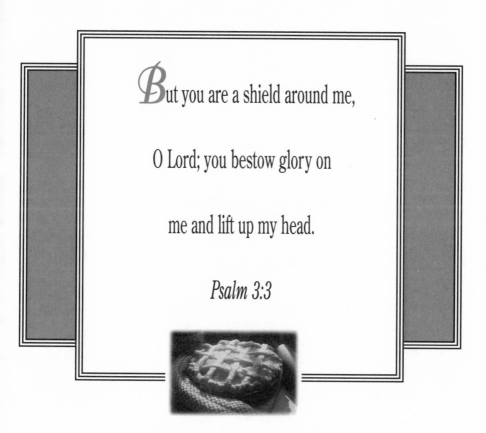

*B*ut you are a shield around me,

O Lord; you bestow glory on

me and lift up my head.

Psalm 3:3

····Mama's Rules for Livin'····

87.

*G*et rid of all bitterness.

"I" is the key difference between a person who is bitter or better.

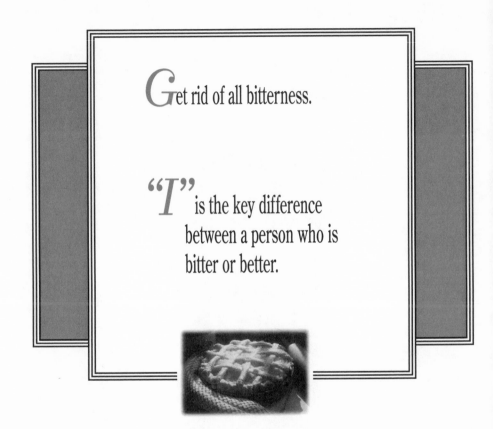

*T*he person who is always

harping on something is not

necessarily an angel.

····Mama's Rules for Livin'····

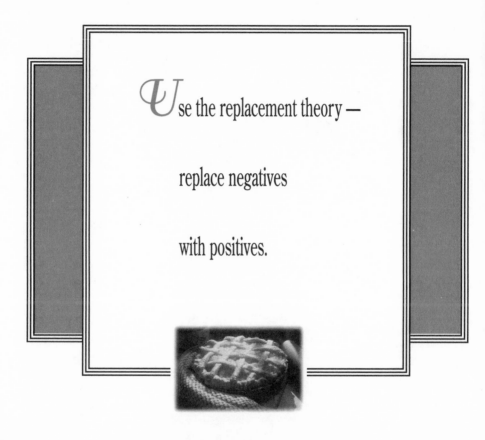

$\mathcal{U}$se the replacement theory —

replace negatives

with positives.

····Mama's Rules for Livin'····

*W*hen you become a parent

remember: Tell your children you love,

appreciate, and believe in them.

*T*hink quality in all you do.

*I*f it is right, it deserves your
best effort.

····**Mama's Rules for Livin'**····

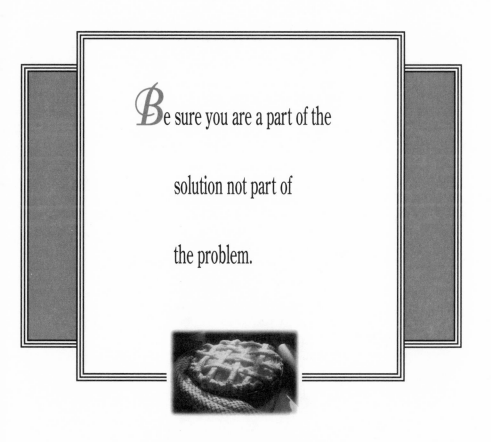

$\mathcal{B}$e sure you are a part of the

solution not part of

the problem.

*R*emind yourself — I've come
a long way.

*E*ncouragement refreshes
the spirit.

····*Mama's Rules for Livin'*····

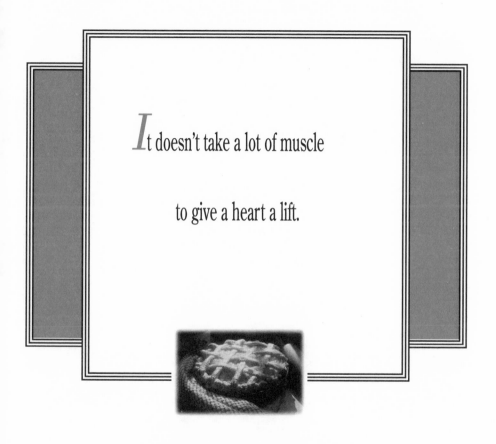

*I*t doesn't take a lot of muscle

to give a heart a lift.

You are the only one who has

your talents and abilities.

····*Mama's Rules for Livin'*····

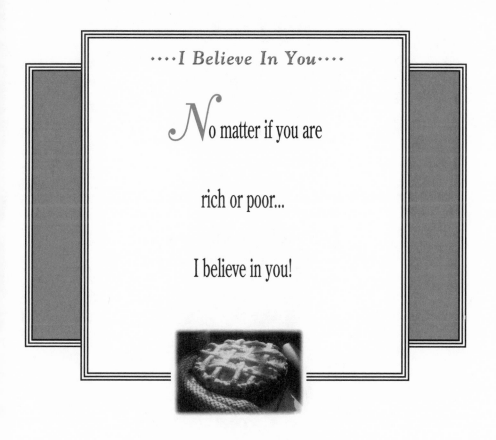

····*I Believe In You*····

*N*o matter if you are

rich or poor...

I believe in you!

*U*se the most powerful card
you own — your library card.

*T*he greatest unexplored area
lies underneath your hat.

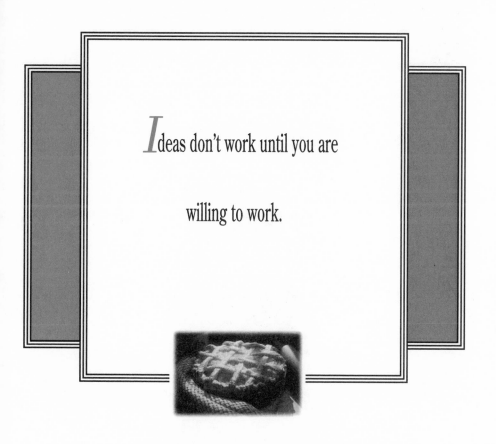

*I*deas don't work until you are

willing to work.

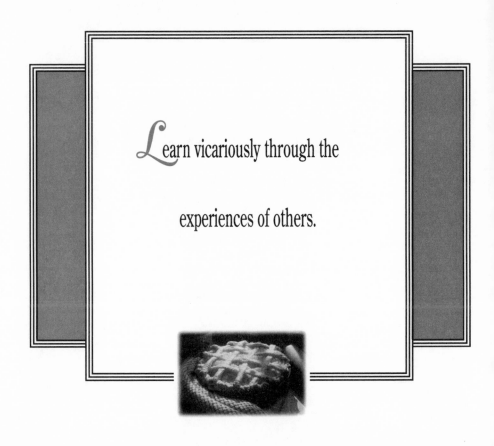

$\mathcal{L}$earn vicariously through the

experiences of others.

*D*etermine to be a world-class

person, capable of operating

in any arena of life...

never quit!

*W*e become like the people
with whom we associate.

*S*elect your mentors carefully.

····*Mama's Rules for Livin'*····

Concentrate on small

improvements.

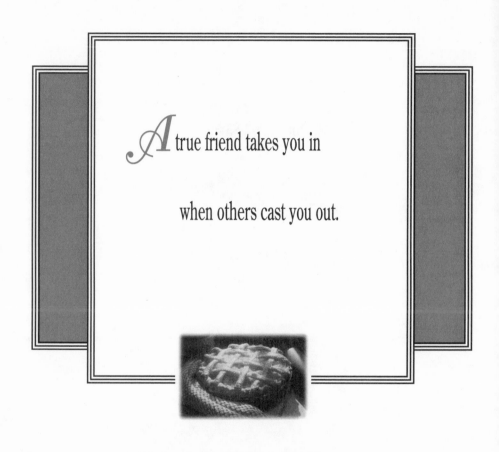

A true friend takes you in

when others cast you out.

····*Fight For The Underdog*····

*P*eople tend to favor underdogs

but follow top dogs...fight

for the underdog anyway!

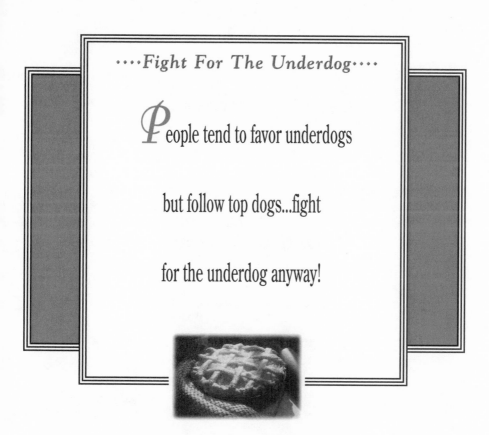

····*Mama's Rules for Livin'*····

*C*onsider — how will you put
your life together?

*G*oals are your roadmap to
success.

Goals, like eggs, soon spoil

unless hatched.

····Mama's Rules for Livin'····

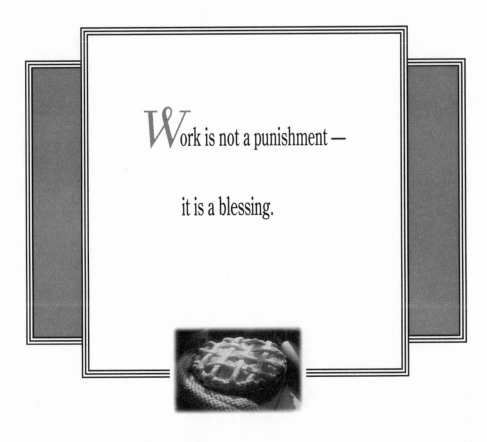

$\mathcal{W}$ork is not a punishment —

it is a blessing.

*W*hatever your hand finds to do,

do it with all your might....

Ecclesiastes 9:10

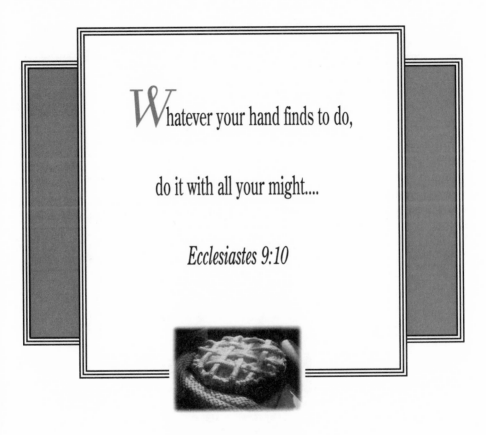

·····Mama's Rules for Livin'·····

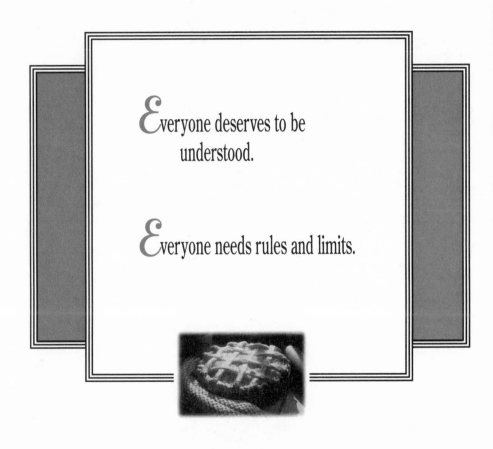

$\mathcal{E}$veryone deserves to be
understood.

$\mathcal{E}$veryone needs rules and limits.

····Mama's Rules for Livin'····

$\mathcal{Y}$ou cannot help a person

uphill without getting

closer to the top yourself.

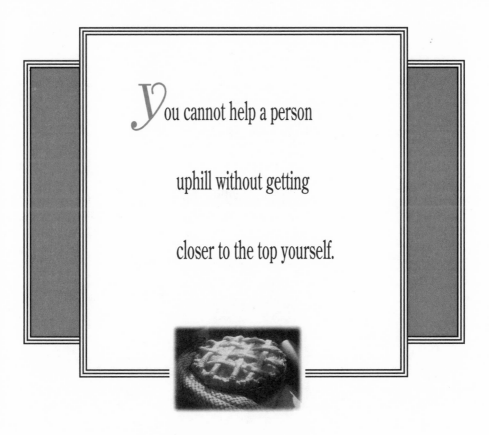

*M*aking a mistake is not an

excuse for living a mistake.

····Mama's Rules for Livin'····

When you become a parent

remember: Our children's

values will lay the foundation

for tomorrow's world.

$\mathcal{L}$ife is not always fair.

$\mathcal{D}$on't worry about what
you cannot control.

····Mama's Rules for Livin'····

$y$ou can have anything you want

but not everything you want.

••••*Mama's Rules for Livin'*••••

*A*ttitudes are contagious.

A positive attitude will have
positive results.

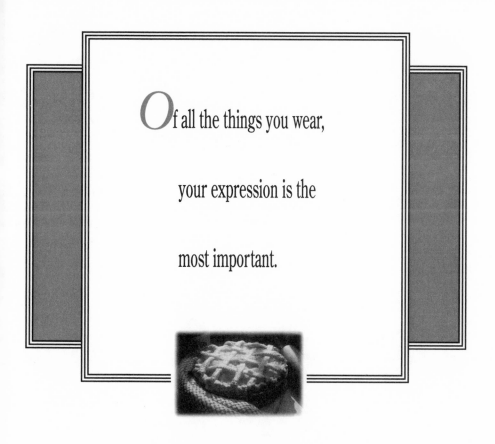

*O*f all the things you wear,

your expression is the

most important.

·····**Mama's Rules for Livin'**·····

117.

*I*f anyone speaks badly of you,

live so no one will believe it.

····Mama's Rules for Livin'····

118.

····I Believe In You····

*N*o matter what others say...

I believe in you!

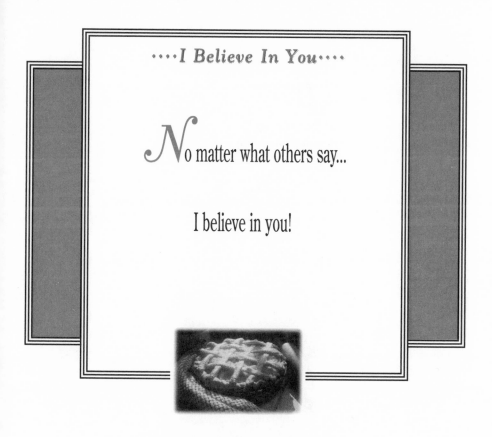

····Mama's Rules for Livin'····

119.

*P*ain is inevitable —
misery is a choice.

*F*orgive.

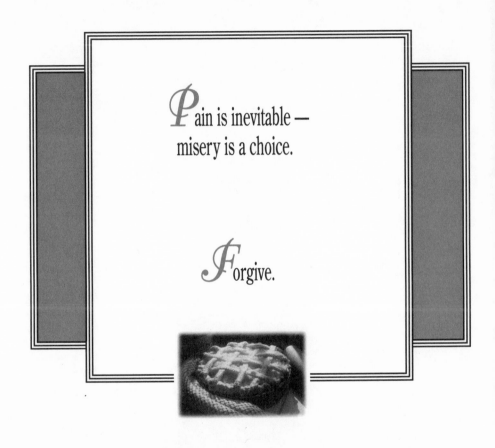

····**Mama's Rules for Livin'**····

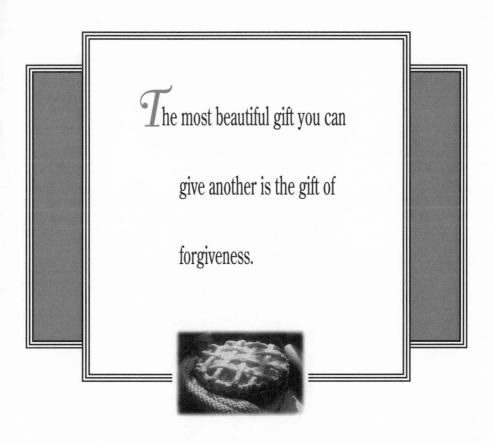

$\mathcal{T}$he most beautiful gift you can

give another is the gift of

forgiveness.

····Mama's Rules for Livin'····

*I*t is better to wear out than

to rust out.

····**Mama's Rules for Livin'**····

····Never Quit····

*F*ailure and defeat become

permanent only when we

quit trying...never quit!

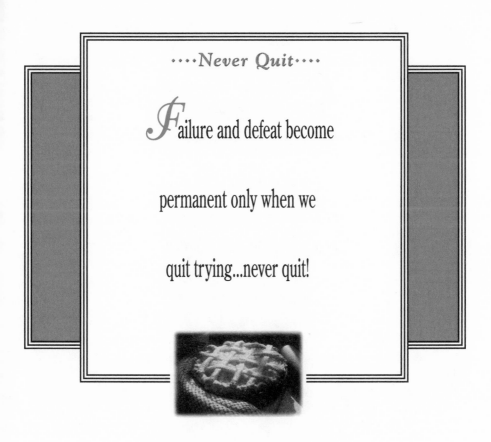

····Mama's Rules for Livin'····

*K*indness is a language
everyone understands.

*S*andwich criticism between
thick layers of praise.

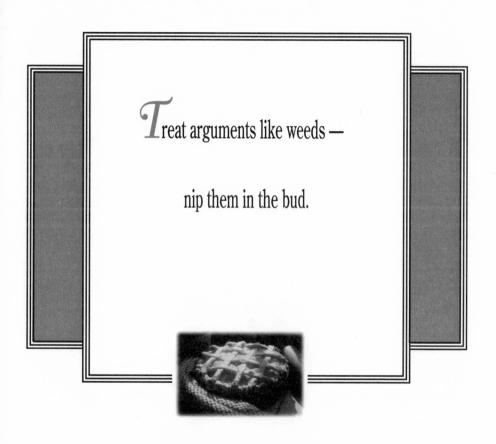

*T*reat arguments like weeds —

nip them in the bud.

·····Mama's Rules for Livin'·····

125.

What is down in your well

comes up in your bucket.

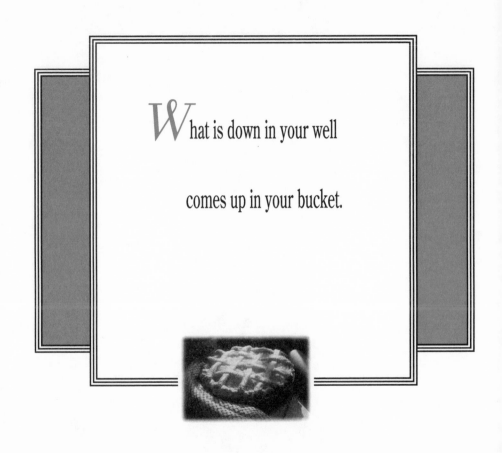

···· **Be Honest And Frank** ····

*H*onesty and frankness will

make you vulnerable...

be honest and frank anyway!

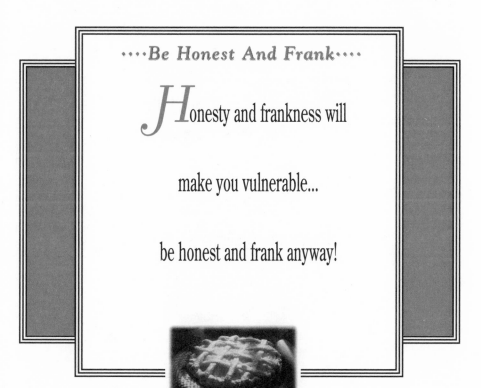

···· **Mama's Rules for Livin'** ····

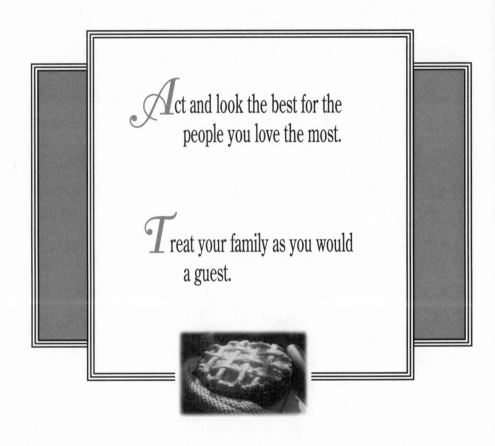

*A*ct and look the best for the
people you love the most.

*T*reat your family as you would
a guest.

····Mama's Rules for Livin'····

128.

*S*pend time with people who

are for you.

····Mama's Rules for Livin'····

129.

*G*ratitude is the memory

of your heart.

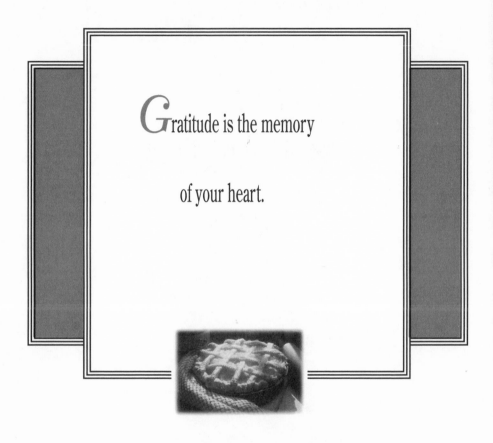

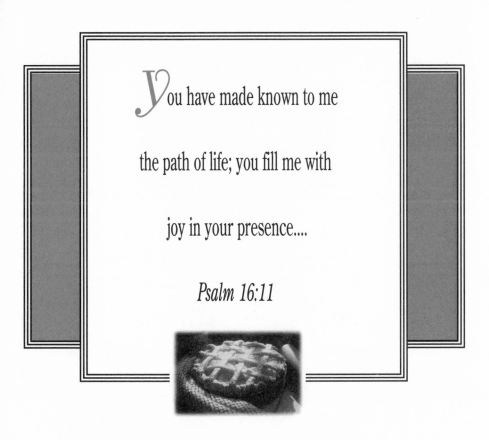

$\mathcal{Y}$ou have made known to me

the path of life; you fill me with

joy in your presence....

Psalm 16:11

····Mama's Rules for Livin'····

Jesus is the best model for your home and marriage.

God is the perfect parent.

*I*f you wish to be loved, love!

····Mama's Rules for Livin'····

Get it together, then remember

where you put it!

····**When You Become A Parent**····

W hen you become a parent
remember: The best way to
keep children at home is to
make the home pleasant and
a place they feel loved —
and let the air out of their tires!

····**Mama's Rules for Livin'**····

135.

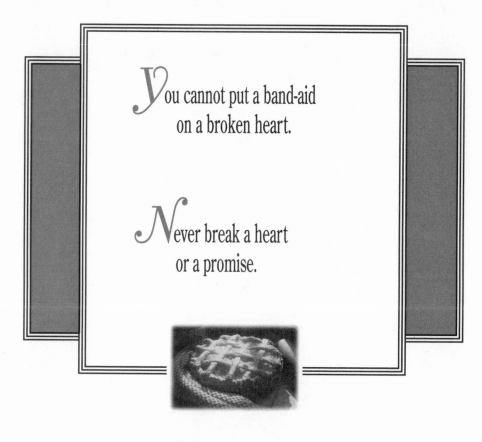

*Y*ou cannot put a band-aid
on a broken heart.

*N*ever break a heart
or a promise.

····*Mama's Rules for Livin'*····

$\mathcal{N}$ever jest about another's

faults, failures, misfortunes,

or handicaps.

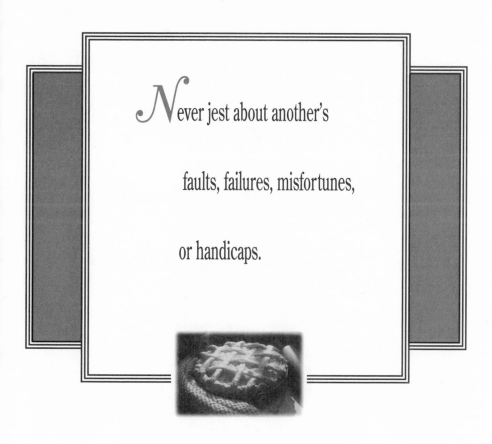

God may not always call
the qualified.

God always qualifies the called.

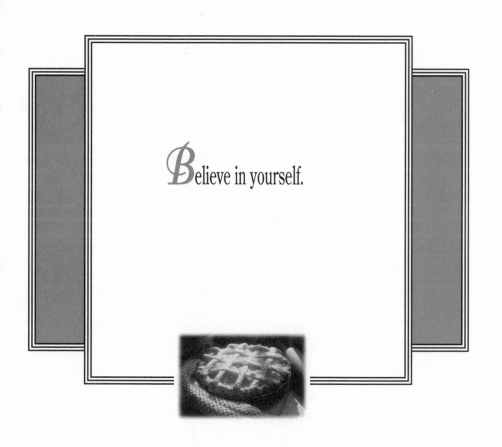

$\mathcal{B}$elieve in yourself.

····Mama's Rules for Livin'····

139.

Don't let yesterday's failures

bankrupt today's efforts.

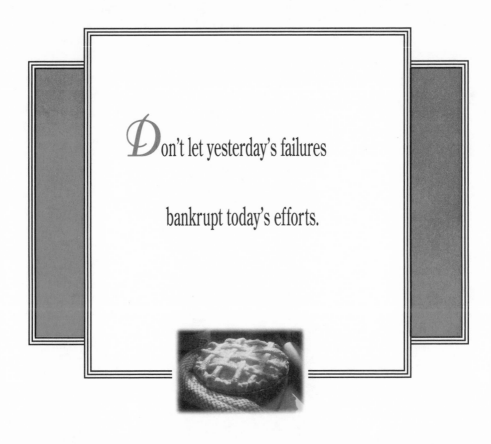

····Mama's Rules for Livin'····

140.

*N*o matter, no matter,

no matter...

I believe in you!

𝒴ou are "thumb body."

𝒴ou are a child of God.

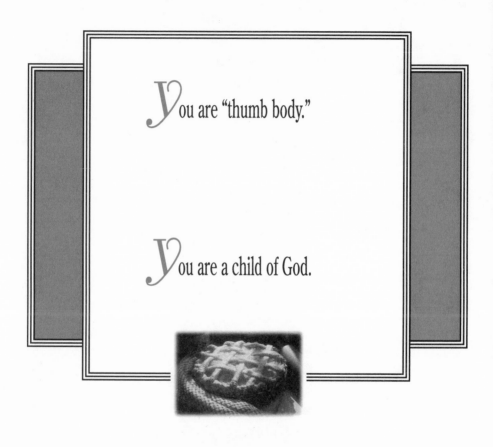

$\mathcal{R}$ecognize that your performance

will always be consistent with

the way you see yourself.

····**Mama's Rules for Livin'**····

143.

*P*roblems become smaller when

you embrace them as a

part of life.

····**Mama's Rules for Livin'**····

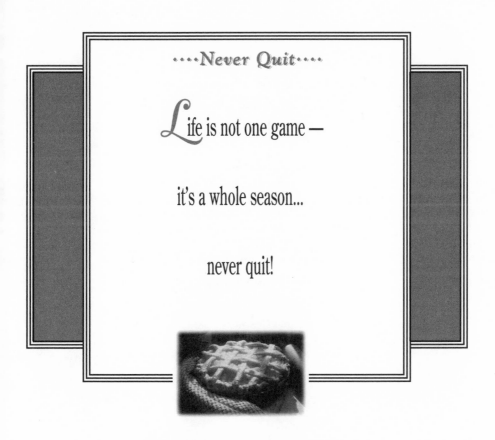

····Never Quit····

$\mathcal{L}$ife is not one game —

it's a whole season...

never quit!

····Mama's Rules for Livin'····

145.

*R*emember that we become real
through love, maturity, and
understanding.

*T*hings invisible to the eye
are the most important.

*T*he largest room in the world

is the room for improvement.

·····Mama's Rules for Livin'·····

147.

We all need love — especially

when we do not deserve it.

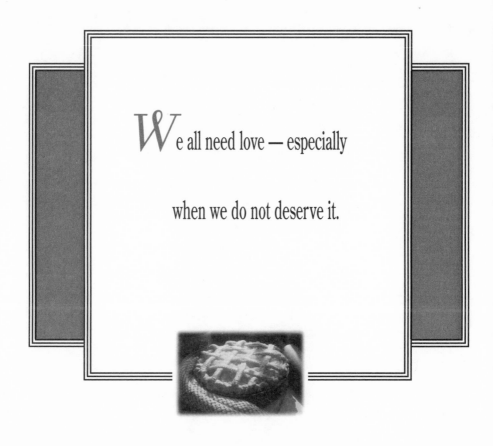

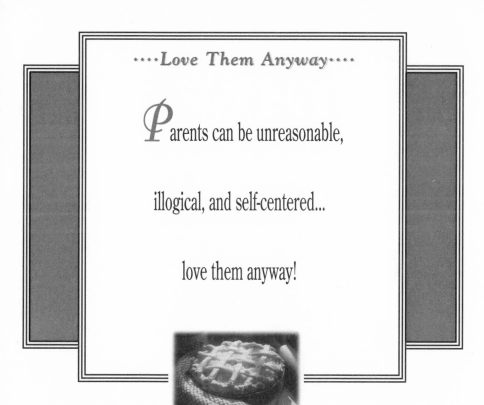

····Love Them Anyway····

*P*arents can be unreasonable,

illogical, and self-centered...

love them anyway!

····Mama's Rules for Livin'····

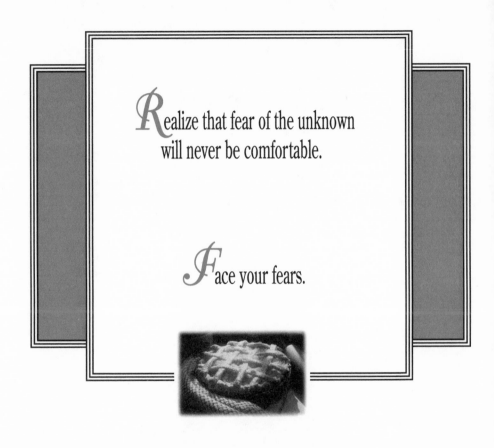

*R*ealize that fear of the unknown
will never be comfortable.

*F*ace your fears.

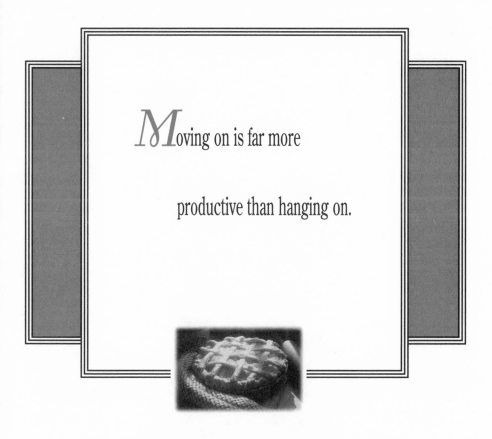

Moving on is far more

productive than hanging on.

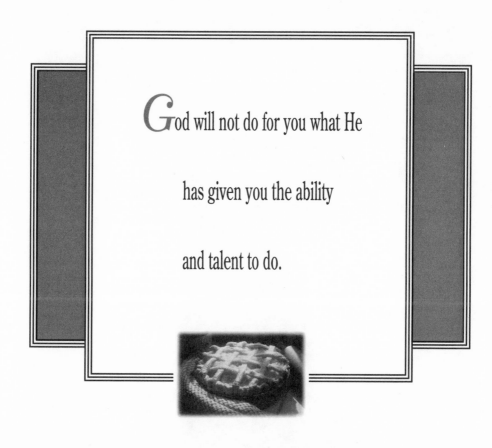

God will not do for you what He

has given you the ability

and talent to do.

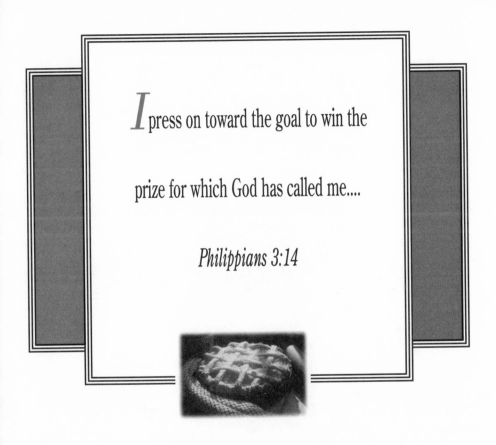

I press on toward the goal to win the

prize for which God has called me....

Philippians 3:14

····Mama's Rules for Livin'····

153.

$\mathcal{L}$ittle is much when God is in it.

$\mathcal{R}$emember your label:
"Made by God."

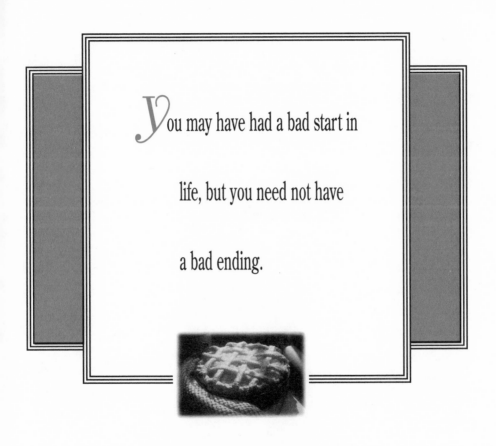

$y$ou may have had a bad start in

life, but you need not have

a bad ending.

····Mama's Rules for Livin'····

155.

*I*t isn't *what* happens to you, it's

what you *make* of what

happens to you that makes

the difference.

When you become a parent

remember: If raising children

was going to be easy, it wouldn't

have started off with labor.

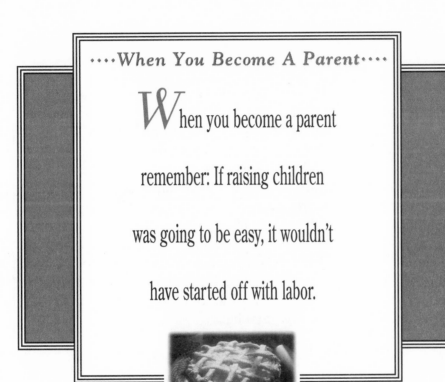

About the Author

Mamie McCullough is one of the country's most popular motivational speakers and has the unique ministry of being an encourager. She addresses tens of thousands of people yearly at churches, schools, and businesses. Having once toured with Zig Ziglar, the "I Can" lady now shares life-changing principles that are instrumental in providing women with ideas, suggestions, insights, and facts on how to raise "great" children. Creator of a course for schools which has reached more than two million students in more than 5,000 schools and author of several books, Mamie feels her greatest achievement in life was receiving her M.A.M.A. degree. The mother of three, she lives in Dallas, Texas, with her husband Herschel.

Other titles by Mamie McCullough include:
I Can. You Can Too!
Get it Together and Remember Where You Put It

To contact the author for your
complimentary copy of her newsletter, *The Encourager*,
write or call:

Mamie McCullough
305 Spring Creek Village
P.O. Box 372
Dallas, Texas 75248
1-800-255-4226

Additional copies of this book and other portable
book titles from **HONOR BOOKS** are
available at your local bookstore.

God's Little Instruction Book Series by Honor Books
How To Be an Up Person in a Down World by Honor Books
Don't Wait for Your Ship To Come In by Honor Books
The Making of a Champion by Mike Murdock
Leadership 101 by John Maxwell
Momentum Builders by John Mason
Winning 101 by Van Crouch

P.O. Box 55388
Tulsa, Oklahoma 74155